Fabulous Things

Starting Your New Normal

Just Miss Yolonda

November Media Publishing, Chicago IL.

Copyright © 2018 Just Miss Yolonda

All rights reserved. No part of this publication may be reproduced, distributed, or transmitted in any form or by any means, including photocopying, recording, or other electronic or mechanical methods, without the prior written permission of the publisher, except in the case of brief quotations embodied in critical reviews and certain other noncommercial uses permitted by copyright law. For permission requests, write to the publisher, addressed "Attention: Permissions Coordinator," at the email address below.

November Media Publishing
info@novembermediapublishing.com

Ordering Information: Special discounts are available on quantity purchases by corporations, associations, and others. For details, contact the publisher at the email address above.

Printed in the United States of America

Produced & Published by November Media Publishing

ISBN: 978-1-7326897-4-9(Print Copy)

First Edition : September 2018

10 9 8 7 6 5 4 3 2 1

CONTENTS

INTRODUCTION VII

CHAPTER 1: THE BEGINNING 1

CHAPTER 2: GROWING PAINS 13

CHAPTER 3: SHIFT 25

CHAPTER 4: CHANGE 33

CHAPTER 5: GRIEF 35

CHAPTER 6: NEW NORMAL 41

CHAPTER 7: MISTAKES 45

CHAPTER 8: BLOW IT UP AND START AGAIN 49

CHAPTER 9: A NEW JOURNEY BEGINS 53

CHAPTER 10: PERSPECTIVE 65

EPILOGUE 69

ACKNOWLEDGMENTS

First, I want to give honor to God, who is the head of my life, and my Lord and Savior Jesus Christ. I would also like to thank my mother, Leontyne Williams, and my brother, DeWitt C. Williams Jr., for believing in me and this project. I will forever be in your debt. We are making it through one of the hardest tests, but with the help of the Lord, we are making it.

Thank you, Williams and Wilson family for supporting us through the most difficult times of our lives.

Thank you to the church families I've had throughout my life: First Corinthian MB Church, North Chicago, Illinois, Christ Tabernacle MB Church, Rockford, Illinois, New Hope MB Church, DeKalb, Illinois, and the greatest church in the world—the Salem Baptist Church of Chicago. I have grown so much under your ministries and matured into the person that I am today. I thank you.

Thank you to all my divas! To my girls and my crew who have prayed, cried, and encouraged me throughout this writing process, thank you for the long conversations on the phone, reading parts of the book, and rejoicing with me throughout each victory. It's just the beginning. Now it's your turn! Who's next? Who is the next author and business owner?

Thank you to every pastor, minister, big brother, and male figure that has crossed my path. You have all been protectors and prayer warriors and have provided guidance. I am forever grateful.

Finally, this book is dedicated to my father, DeWitt C. Williams Sr., my baby sister, Milynda R. Williams, and my boy, M&M. Thank you for always believing in me and for all the joy, pain, tears, conversations, laughter, and lessons I have learned from each of you. May you continue to rest in the arms of our Lord and Savior. Until we meet again.

INTRODUCTION

If you are finding yourself reading this book, some major loss must have occurred in your life. There are all types of loss: loss of a loved one, situation, job, friendship, divorce, etc. Loss is loss. Let me be the one of many to say, "I am sorry for your loss." It sounds cliché, but from the depths of my heart, I truly am. Loss is something that a plethora of people have tried to describe, but it can never be felt until experienced. Understand and trust that I am not being flippant on this next statement: it will pass. It may take a while, but you will smile, laugh, talk, and move again.

The other thing that they don't tell you about loss is some of the truths you will learn about yourself. Loss will magnify the relevancy of who you are in the scheme of things, once the void in your life has happened. Within your circle or dynamic, everyone plays a role and a character. I don't think we realize the part we play until the character dies off or is written out of our story.

For example, *Scandal* is my favorite television show. I am truly a *Scandal*-holic. When a certain main character dies off in this show or is written out, we have a few questions. Will the show continue? Will it be the same? Will I like it? Shonda (the writer) needs to fix this. Unbeknownst to us, we are part of the show that we didn't sign up for, nor auditioned for. Trust me, people are watching the show of your life. What's interesting is the fact that we ask those questions about a show, but do we ask the same question when a loss has happened and the situation has shifted? How do we carry on?

"To every thing there is season, and a time to every purpose under heaven." (Ecclesiastes 3:1) I received this on many sympathy cards. If the Lord has allowed you another day, take that opportunity to dream again, be again, and start again.

On to the next!!!!

Now it's time to hear my story.

CHAPTER 1

THE BEGINNING

"In the beginning..." (Genesis 1:1)

It was the best day of my life. I mean, the sun was shining, life was perfect for an eighteen-year-old embarking on the greatest moment of an impressionable, yet opinionated young adult. Leaving home, flying the coop—however you say it—I was leaving for college!!!! Can you imagine? Finally leaving this boring suburb of Waukegan and starting my new life as a college student. No rules, college men, parties, away from my parents, and, oh yeah, school... not just school but college. I was off to my *Different World*—that was one of my favorite shows—wondering if my college experience would look like what I saw on television.

May, which is the best month ever, because of my birthday, was a month of celebration. I turned eighteen, prom, birthday party, and graduation. It was the most exciting three weeks, and three months of my life. My H.S. crew, which was affectionately called the Brothers of Brotherly Brotherhood and the Sisters of Sisterly Sisterhood had said our goodbyes, see you laters, and farewells through parties, outings, picnics, dates, Great America, and the final meet up as we went our separate ways.

Goodbyes and/or see you laters were going to be my "new normal" as I navigated this thing called life, but that's a discussion for later.

As I mused over the last three months of my life while packing, my friend Vic from kindergarten showed up with his mother. He was riding down to the "cornfields" of Northern Illinois University with me.

"Londa!!!" my dad bellowed. "That boy is here and it's time to go!! Let's go now so I won't be in traffic. I need to go to work to pay for all of this!!"

"Coming!!" I yelled back excitingly.

I was so excited, because I was the first in my

immediate family to leave the nest. I rushed and looked around my room, reminiscing how fast life moved.

"This is it", I said to myself. "Time to conquer the world and show them what this 90s young lady has to offer."

My mother, sister, and brother were outside by the truck along with my boy Vic and his mother. Hugging my sister first, she proclaimed, "I finally have the room to myself. Don't worry; I will have Momma bring me down as soon as possible. I can't wait to hang with you; I am so over these high school boys!!"

Next, my brother. He never said much, and he didn't disappoint. All he said was, "See you later...," gave me an awkward hug, and left.

Finally, my mother. She hugged me so tight and for so long, it seemed. I felt her emotion through her hug because her crazy middle child was leaving the nest. She always referred to us as her little birds. Right after she hugged me came the laundry list of dos and don'ts I had heard all my life:

"Make sure you call me as soon as you get there and settled."

"Yes, mama," I said.

"Keep your clothes clean."

"Yes mama," I promised.

"If you go to a party, make sure you are not by yourself."

"Yes, mama, I know," I cried.

"If you sit your drink down, don't drink it again, you know what happened to such and such." (Why does your parent always know a so and so or a such and such situation?)

"Yes, mama," I groaned.

"Don't forget to go to church, pay attention in class, call us if you need anything..."

She was about to go on a tangent when my Daddy said, "Enough, Tina. We will never make it on the road."

We got in the truck as Vic said his goodbyes to his

mother, and my mother finally yelled, "And don't bring home no babies!!!"

So embarrassed . . .

My dad, Vic, and I were on our way to the Cornfield to begin new chapters in our lives. We were bumping WGCI with Tom Joyner, the hardest working man on radio, playing the hits. Ecstatic was not the word. The bonus of going to college was that my cousin was a junior at the school, and he was waiting for our arrival.

Once we arrived, it was pure chaos. All types of parents, students, staff, Greek organizations, cheerleaders, etc. greeted us as we checked in. Vic and I lived in the same dorm but on different floors. Our R.A.'s greeted us, and the staff showed us to our rooms while helping us move in. I lived on the eleventh floor with "B visitation." Basically, I had minimal freedom in my living arrangements. That meant boys had to be off the floor by eleven p.m. during the week and could hang out on the weekends. With everything moved in, my dad looked at me, and I could see he was having a hard time.

"Be good; your cousin should be here soon." With that, he walked out the door to leave me to unpack. (I was told later he cried all the way back home.)

I felt lost. My parents had to work and only had time to drop me off. They left me in the capable hands of my crazy cousin James to help me with the process they had no knowledge about. Now let me explain James. He was the director of one of the coldest choirs on NIU campus, he was a member of Alpha Phi Alpha Inc., and he never met a stranger. He could make up his own rules, and everyone seemed to follow them. He had already called to see if I was in the Cornfield and was somehow able to get up to my floor with no problem . . . Don't ask how; he just did.

"Hey cousin," he said. "How much stuff did Aunt Tina send with you?" he groaned. "Did she at least send food? I know I am definitely going to eat here!!!"

We made our introductions, and he grabbed one of my many boxes and dumped it out on my bed.

"Put this away, and I will be back." Now with my

cousin being the director of the choir, he was supposed to be recruiting new members, since he made up his own rules, who knows where he went off to. He came back a half an hour later and dumped another box, examined the contents to see what he could "borrow"—especially my snacks—and said, "I'll be back." That process took place throughout the first four hours of that day.

After everything was in its proper place, James had some other freshmen that he felt I should meet and was going to take us all on a personal tour. He called me later that day and told me, "Get dressed. Meet me in the lobby." *Click*. He never said goodbye he just hung up the phone.

James drove up in his car, and that was the first time I met M&M. Tall brother, handsome, with a big smile. *Not bad* I said to myself. We all piled up in the car and took off on my cousin's crazy tour.

"Hello, young lady, how are you doing?" he drawled like he was from the south. Introductions were made.

"This is M&M from Springfield," James said.

"Springfield?" I inquired. "There's black people out there?" (I could be mean.)

"Be nice," James said.

"The capital of this great state of Illinois," M&M said enthusiastically.

"Nerd," I thought.

"May I ask, where are you from?" M&M asked.

"Waukegan" I said distantly. "Waukegan is down the street from Great America. Maybe you have been to Great America?" I thought to myself, "Nobody knows where Waukegan is."

M&M got very excited and said, "I love Great America, and I've been to the one close to Springfield. It must be very exciting to live so close."

"Not really," I said. James gave me that look again, which meant be nice.

After touring the campus, M&M invited us to his room. While touring with us, M&M shared that it was his birthday, and it was his first birthday away from home and he wanted some company. So, to his dorm we went. There was a boom box in his room, and we turned it to WGCI where Rick Party was bumping the hits for the evening. Small talk was exchanged with everyone in the room. You know, questions like:

What is your name?

Where are you from?

Are you a Christian?

Any siblings?

What's your major/minor?

How will you conquer the world?

What do you want to do?

Why did you choose this school? Etc.

It was at this moment that M&M pulled out a piece a paper that he couldn't wait to share. They were stories about himself and all of his accomplishments. *Bragging*, I thought to myself! It was then he explained his bucket list, as though he had read my thoughts.

"Your bucket list?" I inquired.

"Yes" he stood authoritatively, "my bucket list."

He started reading it, and for the first time I was truly impressed with this skinny country boy. It was at this moment that I realized I had met someone who knew exactly where he wanted to go and would move heaven and earth to get there.

From that moment on M&M and I friendship grew. Our first year in college was not only special, but we lived through some historic moments in life and in television:

- Magic Johnson announced that he contracted HIV
- Rodney King verdict
- Michael Jackson kissed a girl in his video "Remember the Time"
- Steve Urkel turned into Stefan
- Dwayne Wayne interrupted Whitley wedding to Byron (the future Daddy Pope from *Scandal*) and married her.

- We found out who shot Will on *All My Children*, when I got into soap operas
- Chicago Bulls were in the playoffs again

Throughout my freshman year, M&M and I hung out almost every day. I watched the young man begin his journey of taking off items on his bucket list and taking the campus by storm his four years there. We laughed, talked, celebrated, and, yes, fought often, as we navigated through the ups and downs of college life and adulthood. He graduated first and went on to pursue his postgraduate studies and career. I did the same, and we kept up with each other all along the way.

CHAPTER 2

GROWING PAINS

"Grow in grace..." (2 Peter 3:18)

M&M and I were moving along in life into adulthood. You know how it is. First real interview for your adult job, first job, first apartment, and all the responsibilities that come along with them. M&M was so excited because his first job was his first big break. The pay was so great he was able to move to Chicago, where we were back within proximity of each other. Since he had a high-paying job, he had the best connections to every possible concert, function, and of course shopping. While we were in college, I always had every need met and shared my resources with him. Now, at this season of our life, the roles were reversed, and I didn't have it like he did. He had my back like I had his back in college.

Since we talked every day at the same time, our calls would sound like this on weekdays:

Phone rings

"Hey, girl," he'd drawl.

"Hey, big head," I'd say back.

"I got your big head!!!" he'd retort. "What are you doing this weekend?" he'd ask.

"Church, singing, laundry, reflecting on life, bored out of my mind..." I'd mumble. "What do you think?"

"Little girl answer the question." He'd sigh. (I could get under his skin with his impatient self. And "little girl" was the indicator I was working his last nerve.)

"Again," he'd say with a pause, "what are you doing Friday?"

"Nothing!!!" I'd snap.

"I got these tickets, but your response determines *if* I will take you to this concert, because..."

Before he'd continue, I'd interrupt and spit back, "First of all, ain't no one told you to call this here phone." I would be getting worked up. "I don't need to go anywhere with your bald head self. Beeeesides I don't..."

He'd interrupt back and speak in his authoritative voice, when he was tired of my tangent, "It's tickets to see Beyoncé..."

There'd be a pregnant pause.

I'd hurriedly say, "So what time do you want me to be ready? I can be there now. Is it today or tomorrow?"

We'd both laugh, and he'd say, "Crazy girl. Catch the train tomorrow, and be here by seven and we'll hang out."

That's how every conversation began with our adventures. Whether it was concerts, plays, restaurants, or speaking engagements, we were there supporting and rooting for each other. M&M was my number one fan and my favorite encourager. Whenever he had anything huge to attend and needed a date, I was his girl and vice versa. We had annual functions that he always planned. We always went to:

- Gospel fest
- UniverSoul Circus
- Taste of Chicago concerts
- Concerts of all kinds
- Holiday events that required a date
- Each other's Valentine's when there was no one special in our lives
- Six Flags in July!!! I hated the heat, and he would always choose the hottest day of the year. The older we got, the more we wanted to see if we could ride all the roller coasters. Eventually I stopped riding any rides that were in the shape of a circle, it's like the floor would drop. Just watching would make me nauseated.
- Fright Fest at Six Flags

We loved to be scared by anything, plus the atmosphere was electric during that time of the year.

With every trip to Fright Fest, we found out different things about each other. One year M&M found out how competitive I was. We were playing air hockey. M&M started talking smack.

"Little girl, you wanna play?" he quipped. "I will be easy on you since you are a rookie, but I can play this game.

"Oh yeah," I said.

He put money in the machine and said, "I will let you go first, since you so short, and the weaker vessel!!!" He laughed.

I didn't say anything because I was seething. When I hit the puck and got the first goal, I smiled and said sweetly and sarcastically, "I wouldn't do that if I were you," as I hit another goal.

"WHAT?????" he yelled. "It's on like Donkey Kong!!!"

"Such a nerd!!" I wolfed back.

Let's just say we were there for over an hour. Jackets came off; we were sweating, getting loud, talking smack back and forth, catching the attention of people passing by. Music was playing as we played game after game. When we finished, I'd lost to him by one game. He cheered but not for long. He was tired. I laughed for a moment, because I was tired as well.

"Let's get something to drink; I'm hot and winded," he said.

Now the one thing that surprised me about M&M was that he was good at playing the games where you win prizes. The night of the air hockey incident, we went to an area in the park where you can win stuffed animals. I really liked the Tweety Bird I saw. M&M, being the showboat that he was, not only won me that Tweety Bird, but nine other stuffed animals that night. I was smiling from ear to ear; I'd never in my life seen anything like it. None of my ex-boyfriends could ever win me any stuffed animals, and so that was a great experience.

M&M was also my singing partner. Could that man sing. Hanging with him was fun because we could sing with each other all the time in the car, while walking, or hanging out. Every year for my birthday he would sing to me, and it was always a cross between a male version of Marilyn Monroe with a little Luther Vandross vibe. I loved Luther Vandross. Every year, I would cry laughing because he would be so over the top with his birthday rendition.

For his birthday, I would sing to him, but it would be so off-key on purpose it would make him laugh. One birthday I surprised him and sang a song to him by his favorite artist of all time, CeCe Winans. He loved her so much. "Alabaster Box" was the song of choice. After that day, he requested that I sing a CeCe Winans song for his birthday from that point on.

M&M was the fixer. When my world came crashing down, he was one of the first people I called.

>*Phone rings*
>
>"M&M," I would whine.
>
>"What's wrong?" He would say.
>
>"This, that, and everything," I would cry.
>
>"You know Yolonda . . ." He would quote at least twenty scripture passages, then tell me, "You are stronger than this. Better is

coming; don't worry about it."

"OK," I would say, sighing, and get myself together.

True to form, this would be the next part of our conversation:

"Get on the train, come to the city, and let's hang out." Or it would be "Wanna go the movies, a concert, or out to eat?" He would try to fix it.

Finally, there were arguments that would break out every time we would go out. Honestly, I never knew what would trigger the disagreements, but they would be doozies, especially in our twenties. By our thirties, I don't know if we grew tired or we just didn't care. The one argument that stands out the most occurred the day I cooked for him in his new condo. From what I remember, he kept eating out and never cooked in his place, so we would celebrate his new job and condo by staying in. Plus, where he lived, parking was horrible. Setting up to cook, I had my own rhythm. Then here he comes into the kitchen rearranging everything I set up.

Ever the perfectionist, he would ask a million questions on the way I flowed in the kitchen. Now he couldn't cook at the time but was the authority of how it was supposed to be done. He said things like, "My granny doesn't cook it like that" or "My granny uses this seasoning."

I said under my breath, "Then why isn't your granny here in this here kitchen?" I was so upset, because I could cook, and this was a favor to him. When I got to the highest level of being pist, I would get quiet and plot. Finishing cooking, while his back was turned, I fixed my plate. He said something else smart to me, and that was the straw that broke the camel's back. I quickly added an extra concoction that didn't go with nothing that I'd prepared, I stirred it up and made his plate. My momma use to say—since he was quoting his granny—don't make the cook mad.

We sat down and prayed. Yes, we did pray, and I watched as he took his first bite.

"YOLONDA!!!!!" he yelled. I think his mouth was on fire. "WHAT IS THIS??!?!?!"

"Your plate of food," I said calmly and smiling. "Don't you ever interfere with what I am doing, you ARE NOT my father. You don't tell me what to do . . ."

It was on then. We were hollering back and forth. Saying things like:

"You make me sick."

"Leave me alone."

"Don't talk to me."

"I'm out of here; I don't have to take this."

And there were some other colorful words that were said between us that I really can't share. Plus, I don't say those things anymore . . . well . . . often. *smiles*

For two days or more, depending on the argument, there would be no communication between us. At work on the computer, an email would pop up.

"Hey," he wrote.

"What?" I replied.

"Don't be like that," he wrote back.

"What do you want?" I replied.

"I'm sorry," he wrote.

"I'm not," I wrote, smiling to myself.

"C'mon little girl. Stop playing. We both were wrong, and I apologize for my part." He wrote back.

I made him wait twenty minutes, because I was mean and on a call.

"OK. I accept your apology because you are ugly, nobody likes you, and you need my friendship. *smile* (smile)" I wrote back laughing.

"Call me on your lunch, crazy girl; I swear you are going to age me," he wrote back.

"Alright, but I keep you alive," I wrote back.

He would always try to keep the peace between us. He would always come back and get me and try to make things right. Truly, I was the spoiled one in the relationship.

One day, while hanging out, I asked him a very serious question. My friends and M&M could attest that I am very inquisitive and would ask question to hear their point of view with no backlash. I asked him, why are you my friend. The answer he gave, I will not share—it was very personal. But what would happen next, I was not prepared for.

CHAPTER 3

SHIFT

"Time to be born, and a time to die; a time to plant, and a time to pluck up that which is planted" (Ecclesiastes 3:2)

It was 2010, and it was one of those strange years that you would never want to relive again. From beginning to end there was a shift in the air that no one could explain. Everything that I knew that was, was no more. What was right became left, up was down—transition in the worst way. Almost every week of this year, there was a funeral of someone that was prominent in my life. Crazy situations that changed lifestyles became the norm. M&M and I felt this shift. We had the argument of all arguments. It was a doozy, and I told him I needed a minute to collect my thoughts. Youthful arguments are nothing compared to the disagreements of a curve ball, (something that happens that tests the true nature of friendship). We tried to work it out by avoiding the conversation that we needed to have.

Looking back, we were still young and believed at the time avoidance was the best way to keep peace, not knowing it was killing the bond we had. Everything was dying around me and so was our bond. We went to see *Dream Girls* and our rhythm was off. What would usually transpire in our flow just fell into uncomfortable silence. Nineteen years of friendship were hanging in the balance, and I decided I needed space. Phone conversations dwindled down to three times a week. We didn't fuss, just polite conversation.

I was dating again and of course M&M didn't approve. It would be our last argument. It wasn't a yelling match, just a very calm discussion that ended on a soft note. He tried to fix our problem, but I couldn't deal with him; I had to move alone.

"It's the most wonderful time of the year"

It was October, my favorite time of the year. Starting from October 1 through to December 31, it's just one party after another. My favorite season, when the celebrations and the atmosphere are at an all-time high. I love the fall and the winter. There is something magical that happens during this time of year. Can you feel it? There's Halloween, where I enjoy the food, candy, haunted houses, scary things. (Don't tell my church friends.) Then there's Thanksgiving. The only time you can get my family to come together, laugh, talk, sing, and debate . . . yes debate. (That's another book.) Christmas!!!! Yes, Christmas. Church plays, services, singing, cooking, eating, Christmas songs, cookies . . . that feeling and New Year's Eve, the crème de la crème . . . Then everything that I knew... changed!

M&M and I hadn't spoken throughout this time until November, just before Thanksgiving. The relationship I was in ended, and it hurt my feelings. Staring at the phone, I wanted to make the call I always made when something didn't go right. I needed him, but I was too hurt. pride stepped in for two days, and then I couldn't stand it. I called him.

"Hey, girl," he drawled.

"Hey," I said.

"It's been a minute," he said quietly.

At this time, six months had passed with no communication between us. I did miss him. In my mind I didn't want to talk about the issue between us. We would one day, but not that day.

"He broke your heart, didn't he?" he stated.

"You already know," I said.

Silence. I just knew he was about to go into his tangent. Instead, he shifted gears.

"I miss you, and I know I hurt you. But know we are always friends."

"I know," I said.

Our conversations over the next few weeks were about the happenings between us the previous six months. He told me about his family, what he was doing for the holidays, and his life. I shared with him about getting my masters, my classes, "the jerk," as we named my ex-boyfriend, how I learned to cook, and my precious kitchen gadgets. We talked for hours about my family and everything in between those next three weeks.

"Let's hang out!!!" he said.

Reluctantly, I said, "I don't know."

"I will take you to see the lights after Christmas..." he said, excited. He knew that was my weakness; I love seeing the lights at Christmastime in downtown Chicago.

"YES!!!!" I said, laughing. "You're going home?" I asked.

"Yep," he said. "We will hook up after Christmas, and I have a big surprise for you," he said with a smile in his voice.

It was December 24 and I had to sing at a Christmas program, and "O Holy Night" was the song of choice. That day felt weird. I hadn't heard from M&M. We were working on rebuilding our friendship. He had always called me on December 24 on his way home for the holidays since we were eighteen years old. A nineteen-year tradition and nothing... There was a snowstorm that day, and I thought he'd decided to wait. Finishing up the Christmas dinner and getting dressed for the program, I didn't hear from him. That was not like him. Once I got home and hung out with the family, I fell asleep.

December 25, 2010 at approximately two in the morning I received one of the worst calls in my life. My cousin, who always pranks me when he travels, has an unusual knack for contacting me at crazy times to wish me Merry Christmas.

He called, and I woke up. Seeing his number, I laughed and said, "Merry Christmas!!!!! I finally beat you!!"

Silence. He said to me, "It's M&M. He was killed in a car accident yesterday on his way home for the holidays..."

I was strangely calm, yet in denial. This could not be happening. We had plans. We made plans. We made plans for right after the holidays. We were supposed to grow old together... This could not be happening. WHAT ARE YOU SAYING TO ME???

What you don't know about me, is I say the craziest thing when I am in shock.

I told my cousin, "No that's not true. Facebook didn't say it." It must be someone else, I reasoned within myself. Not him, not a car accident. "Where's my computer; this is not happening."

I have been in seven car accidents and walked away from all of them. This was his first car accident, the first one that I could remember, and he's gone? "No!!!" I yelled. "It must be mistaken identity." I could not breathe.

My cousin stayed calm. He said, "It's true."

While he was explaining, I went to his page only to find out: he's gone.

CHAPTER 4

CHANGE . . .

That's what happened. His funeral came on December 31, 2010. My friend came with me to his funeral. Going to a funeral is always a unique experience. My father says that our brains are like computers. They store a lot of information, good and bad, but just when you need it the most, it pops up in your mind like it just happened. That's how I feel about funerals. Memories come out of nowhere. As I walked into the church and saw his loved ones, mutual friends, enemies—yes enemies—our conversations about his life became real. I met former teachers he boasted about, colleagues, fraternity brothers—his whole life represented within this edifice. During the service, after viewing his body, my mind couldn't help but drift back to our very first encounter. *This is not real*, I kept saying to myself. This person who was the most productive person I've ever known is gone? The one who believed and encouraged me throughout every battle I faced, we part ways here? This early? The service kept on going, and amid it I remembered every good, bad, and indifferent thing that happened to us. Every argument and even our current disagreement that wasn't resolved. I thought I had time. We would have gotten through it, if we only had time.

The choir was now singing. Resolutions were read. People spoke well of him. I sat there with just the memories. Christmas and New Year's were our holidays. We were supposed to do what we always did after Christmas. But fate changed the course. Instead of a buddy day, I had to say goodbye to my buddy. Tornado horns began sounding. I couldn't say goodbye properly because we had to leave in a hurry. A tornado was making its way to the town. "So long, sir. See you later," I said to him. Not knowing that the tornado of my life was about to change everything.

January 1, 2011 my "new normal" started.

CHAPTER 5

GRIEF

"A time to weep, and a time to laugh; a time to mourn, and a time to dance" (Ecclesiastes 3:4)

According to BetterHelp.com there are seven stages of grief:

1. Shock—Initial paralysis at hearing bad news
2. Denial—Trying to avoid the inevitable
3. Anger—Frustrated outpouring of emotions bottled up
4. Bargaining—Seeking in vain a way out
5. Depression—Final realization of the inevitable

6. Testing—Seeking realistic solutions
7. Acceptance—Finally finding the way forward

Grief is not a fun process, but a necessary one. This book's goal is not to avoid the process of grief. On the contrary, it's a different approach to pick up the pieces to your regularly scheduled program of life. A new season has come; things have changed.

The first few months after M&M's death were the worst. Understand M&M was in my life since the first week I arrived at college. He was the first person I met there. He had accomplished many great things, and I was his sidekick friend. We went everywhere and did almost everything together. Every success or failure we faced together. No romantic love, just a great friend that I talked with every day and now he was gone. He knew everything about me. I talked with him every day at his job from ten to eleven and we would occasionally talk in the evening. From ten to eleven after his death was the worst. Every second, every minute, within that hour was horrible. The job I had at the time had flexible hours. During that hour I was in bed, burying my head under the covers crying. Calling other people to fill the void, but to no avail, was disastrous. M&M knew exactly what to do when I was upset. After his death it was so lonely. It felt like no matter what everyone else tried to do, they couldn't fix it. I just hurt, then I cried, then hurt some more. The Lord and I had many conversations, because He was, and is always the answer. I wasn't angry; I understood what the Bible said about everybody having an appointed time, but my M&M was precious to me. Eventually people became distant, for whatever reason, and that didn't help this process.

Let's not talk about future plans. M&M loved this gospel group that were separated at the time of his death. He knew that they would reunite and tour again. We had a bet and planned on going to their first concert, if they reunited again. Two months after his death, the gospel duo reunited and started touring again. Talk about devastation!!! Memories were everywhere. It felt horrible at first. At this point I questioned God, "How can I continue without him? Who will love me like that? Will I ever recover from this pain?"

My birthday month was five months after M&M's death. Talk about depressing. Our birthday months were the best. We always planned an outing, and we would sing to each other in the craziest fashion. During my birthday month, another tragedy hit: my father had become extremely ill. I prayed daily to God to heal my father, because it looked like I was about to lose him too. I sat there waiting. Waiting for what? M&M to fix this mess he made. It sounds crazy, but I wanted him to fix this. I was waiting for him to come and fix his dying, this pain, this heartache, like he'd always done in the past. I started to get angry because he always fixed it, even without asking me first. I had a flashback that stood out while in prayer. He was a planner to the tenth degree. He planned *everything* in my life, it felt like at times... it was so nerve wrecking. Then the realization came. He wasn't there anymore! The other horrible realization was, I was "that woman" that I thought I wasn't. Have you ever watched one of those *Lifetime* movies where, when the man dies, the wife is clueless? She doesn't know how to do anything or where anything is. She's lost. Well . . . hello, my name was "clueless and lost". He was my scapegoat, the planner, my social life. He planned and paid for everything!!! Man, I didn't know what I'd had. I didn't know how to get tickets to anything, I didn't know how valet parking worked, I just didn't know. I WAS VERY SPOILED!!! I had to get up and move on with my life, while learning how to make myself happy. I had to get up again.

CHAPTER 6

❖

NEW NORMAL

"A time to kill, and a time to heal; a time to break down, and a time to build up" (Ecclesiastes 3:3)

"Life goes on" is so cliché to say, but it's true. I remember the first time I experienced a loss. It was so traumatic to me because I learned death was quick and can happen in an instant. After this death, I looked around my world and nothing stopped. As painful as it felt, McDonald's was still open, TV shows still came on, and school was still in session. I wanted to yell to the whole world, "STOP!!!! Can't you see I lost someone I loved!!! It hurts, and you keep moving???" Yes, we must keep moving. The person and/or the situation is over, but you have another day. Another chance. Another opportunity.

While in prayer, I remembered M&M's bucket list. His bucket list was amazing. He shared with me everything he was going to accomplish before his death. Why did this list pop up in my head? Maybe because at that moment I became inspired by the fact that he moved strategically through life with a plan in mind, accomplishing every goal he set out to do. Then I thought, *what if I stepped out to do my dreams*? Was it too late? He had no idea that at thirty-seven the curtain would close on his performance of this thing called life, and he had truly finished his course. My mind drifted to one of my favorite quotes, about graveyards, by Les Brown. I quote this quite often to people afraid to live:

> The graveyard is the richest place on earth, because it is here that you will find all the hopes and dreams that were never fulfilled, the books that were never written, the songs that were never sung, the inventions that were never shared, the cures that were never discovered, all because someone was too afraid to take that first step, keep with the problem, or determined to carry out their dream.

Bucket list, I thought. "Get up!!!" I said to myself. It's time to live again!

Treasure every lesson I learned from him and keep it moving. One of the most painful things I had to do was pack up all our memories and put them away for another day. I loved him, but this part of my life was now behind me, and I had to move forward into my new normal. My thirty-eighth birthday was coming up, and my partner in crime was no longer here. What should I do? Fabulous Things, the new annual bucket list, was birthed. My life began that day!!!

Here's how I started this new normal:

Step 1: Start on My Birthday

My birthday was the best day to start. It represented the beginning of my life, in my new year.

Step 2: Use My Age

I was turning thirty-eight, and I had one year to do thirty-eight fabulous things.

Step 3: Journal My Adventure

I would purchase a journal or notebook and rate the places I visited or activities I completed and date the entries.

Step 4: Do Something Different

I had only a year to get this done. I had 365 days to make it happen.

Step 5: Newness Is Everywhere

This bucket list could be simple, extravagant, cheap, or expensive. The choice was up to me.

There you have it. I had a plan, a purpose, now it was time to move . . .

I WAS SO SCARED!!!!

CHAPTER 7

MISTAKES

"A time to keep, and a time to cast away"
(Ecclesiastes 3:6)

Now at this stage of the game, there was a plan, but how to implement this plan was difficult. Plans often had been made, but there was no execution. The first step is always met with a strong level of doubt. This past weekend, I went ziplining for the first time, officially. Ziplining had been offered at a children's party I'd attended, so I'd gotten a taste of what it felt like. On this day I was on a treetop, forty feet above the ground. (I will never do this again.) My harness was on, safe and secure. The group I was with had learned the proper procedures and protocols to ensure our safety. After a few obstacles courses to get to the zipline part, it was time to take the first step off the treetop to zipline. Not just any step, but a step off one of the highest trees. A friend of mine, who was behind me, had to coach me to take that first step. He said that the harness had me safe and secure, that I would not fall, to just sit and jump." JUST SIT AND JUMP!!!!! *Do you see what I see?* I said to myself. I have to trust something to carry me to the next location? There was no turning back. I had to have faith in the process.

This new normal is part of the process. There is no going back to business as usual. That is your past, filled with good and bad memories. Life is full of change. It's not easy, but you must take that first step. Honestly, you may go kicking and screaming, like I did when I stepped off that treetop. (Yes . . . I hollered). But what a thrill to step out into the unknown and experience something different.

Unfortunately, I have seen both sides of the reaction to death. Not to sound too judgmental, but from my experience, staying stuck is not a pretty picture. All of us handle death differently, but to stay at the grave site is not my cup of tea. I believe that my loved ones would want me to remember them fondly but to also move on. Life is short is not just a truism, but something as a people we should take seriously. Let me be the first to say, this journey can open new doors. Insanity is doing the same thing repeatedly, expecting different results. That's what happened the first time I tried to implement this new strategy. I tried to do everything at first, just like M&M and I used to do. I discovered a couple of things:

1. It didn't feel the same. I was miserable, because I could see us everywhere. I walked out, ran out of so many places, very upset. Some places, I didn't get to the door because of the memories. Eventually, I was able to, but that took time.

2. The places I could go to, I realized, I didn't like as much as I thought. If I was being honest, I had tolerated some of our experiences. They were OK when we were together, but by myself, absolutely not. I blew up the plan and started the journey over again.

With this new outlook, I continued to rediscover my life. After the initial defeat, I had to readjust my surroundings. The first thing I did to help me move on, which was difficult at first, was to pack away all the memories in my living space. We had pictures galore. I had gifts from him for every birthday, holiday, or just because. I couldn't sit in those memories and be healthy. It hurt too much. I put them away, gently, and started my new course.

Goodnight, M&M. I truly miss you, but I need to live again.

CHAPTER 8

❖

BLOW IT UP AND START AGAIN

"And no man putteth new wine into old bottles: else the new wine doth burst the bottles, and the wine is spilled, and the bottles will be marred: but new wine must be put into new bottles." (Mark 2:22)

Pulling out my journal, I had to decipher how to make this process work. I reread the rules, to make the new normal work. Here's what I wrote in my journal to fix my horrible mistake.

STEP 1: START ON MY BIRTHDAY

OK, I tried that but, failed. Lying to myself by doing the same thing I had always done didn't work. In July, start over again.

STEP 2: USE MY AGE

Thirty-eight things!!!!!! That's impossible. I cannot do thirty-eight new things in 365 days . . . please!! Yes, you can.

STEP 3: JOURNAL MY ADVENTURE

This I can do. I love journaling and journals.

STEP 4: DO SOMETHING DIFFERENT

This was very hard. Looking back, I know why I was somewhat miserable. There was no growth with me, because I was scared to try anything new. I fussed about doing, eating, going, receiving anything different. I was comfortable, complacent, and stuck. My mindset needed an adjustment. My new motto was to be comfortable with being uncomfortable. (That's what my friend Reese's Cup would say). Comfort can be an enemy if you allow it to be. People don't expand their minds because it will make them have to readjust their lifestyle. It's like a merry-go-round, moving, going through the ups and downs of life, but seeing the same thing repeatedly. The spirit of redundancy with the same music, people, places, and things.

STEP 5: NEWNESS IS EVERYWHERE

This is a little harder to accept. If I asked you a few questions or made some statements, you too can see newness everywhere. Newness is like playing spades (don't tell my church friends): either you have a good hand or a bad one. It all depends on who is playing that round.

PERCEPTION. I guarantee, if you look around, there are things you have seen a million times and have questioned it. After looking at that concept a million times, a person can chalk it up as a fleeting thought and keep moving. How many times have you been invited to something new to you and come with some lame excuse for not going. For example, "Wanna try this new Mexican restaurant?" You say, "Naw, it might give me gas," or "I ate food like that before and got the runs," or "They don't cook their food right," or my personal favorite response, "I'm allergic to everything in there." We miss out on growth because of fear, uncertainty, and plain stupidity.

Here's how it worked for me. I drive a lot around the city and the state. When driving, I notice signs, stores, and restaurants. While in the car, questions always plagued my mind: *I need to try that restaurant, store, landmark.* Now, I said this *every time* I passed by these places, but I *never* stopped. So that's where my journey began.

I STOPPED . . .

CHAPTER 9

❖

A NEW JOURNEY BEGINS

"Therefore if any man be in Christ, he is a new creature: old things are passed away; behold, all things are become new." (2 Corinthians 5:17)

Writing this part of the book is funny to me in retrospect. Looking back on my first list of Fabulous Things, it started off very lame and then turned into something great. Seven years ago, stepping out was so stressful to me. I am so proud of the woman I have evolved into, but I am laughing at the woman that started this journey. If you know me or follow me on social media, you know I have done some amazing things. This list is perfect for anyone beginning a new journey. I would compare it to a baby learning how to walk. It looks wobbly at first, but when a child keeps working on it, it becomes second nature. Here is my list. At the end of it, I will tell you about two of my most interesting Fabulous Things. Was I really that scared and stuck in a box? Yes, I was. So here is my first year's journey.

1. Booner's Bar (heard my boy play)
2. Ravinia (Anita Baker)
3. Literature Forum with my favorite author, Beverly Jenkins
4. Black Friday Restaurant
5. Literature Fair
6. Yard House Restaurant
7. UIC Hospital
8. Being a nurse
9. McCathy's Restaurant
10. Dinner by Design
11. Jacksonville, FL
12. Boardwalk in Jacksonville,
13. Navy base

14. Disneyworld Orlando, FL
15. Epcot
16. Animal Kingdom
17. Danced with African drummers and dancers
18. Hollywood Kingdom
19. Auditioned for *American Idol*
20. Won the first show and placed fourth in the finale
21. Magic Kingdom
22. Taught music for eight weeks
23. Planned first vacation
24. Went to see Jeffrey Osborne and Howard Hewitt
25. Sang for Jeffrey Osborne during a concert
26. Ate a fried Twinkie
27. Got a picture of Howard Hewitt

28. Took a picture with Jeffrey Osborne and got his autograph
29. Went to Button Museum
30. Saw Tyler Perry's play twice
31. Went to a gospel concert for free
32. Went to a line-dancing class
33. Tried a new beautician
34. Went to a different church
35. Hoagie Hut
36. Joined Wedding Ministry
37. Went to Natural Hair Expo
38. Went to a funeral of a different race

#19: American Idol at Hollywood Disneyland

One of my ultimate bucket list items had come true: I had gone to Disneyland in Orlando, Florida, for free. It was paid for by a friend. It was the third day of the trip, and he was anxious for me to come to this park and audition for *American*

Idol at Disney. The winner would receive a free fast pass to audition first for the real *American Idol*. I humored him and stood in line to audition. Now keep in mind, I didn't know what the whole process entailed. First, I had to audition in acapella, any song of my choice. I sang the national anthem. One of the workers there said to me, "Be careful, a lot of people mess that song up." I sang the national anthem and won. In my mind, I said, "Good, let's go." Next, the person I auditioned for handed me a paper and headphones. He said, "On your next audition you need to sing two songs to a soundtrack, to see if you will advance to the next round. Now go and practice, and we will call you up."

"The next round?" I cried, giving my friend the evil eye while he laughed. My friend was so excited, but I was annoyed. At this moment, I remembered my Fabulous Things list was lacking things, so I practiced. Two songs by Aretha Franklin stood out, and I practiced both of them as I waited for my audition.

"Yolonda?" said the lady managing the contestants.

"Here I am," I said as I walked hesitantly into the studio.

"Come on in sugar, what's your name?" The Judge said smiling.

"Yolonda," I replied.

"What are we singing today?" He asked.

"'Natural Woman,' and 'Respect,'" I stated. I chose the first because I knew it. The second, I didn't know well, but I told myself I would wing it.

"Alright, Aretha," he said with a smile.

He then pointed to the mic and said, "Stand by the mic and sing the first song." I sang the song, and he made a face.

Uh-oh, I thought. I finished the song, and he shrugged his shoulders.

"Let's try the last song," he said dryly. "Maybe it will be better."

I am not going to lie, he made me mad, dismissing me like that.

He played "Respect." I was already mad: I was angry because I was in a crazy situation, (another book), and I didn't want to be in here anyway—I wanted to see Princess Tiana!!! I really didn't know their version of the song that well; I improvised and personalized the song with a whole attitude. After I sang the last note, everyone in the room started clapping and cheering. "Girl," he hollered, "that's what I was waiting for!!! You made it to the next round!!" he exclaimed

What happened next, I wasn't ready for. Questions were flying out of his assistant's mouth. I received a badge to wear, call time, and where to return. The assistant said I needed to be back so that they could do my hair and makeup, work with my vocal coach, and do a walk-through of the show. I was so glad my friend was there to remember of the instructions.

Since I was a walking advertisement with my badge, we could hang out in the park for three hours before the show.

"A show!!!" I said angrily. Turning to my friend, I said, "Why, why, why did you have me do this?" I exclaimed. Everywhere we went I was treated like royalty. The park knew what the badge I wore meant.

Three hours passed. We showed up, and the process of getting ready for the show began. Whisked away to make-up and hair, I was made over as much as possible for the show. Next, my vocal coach, who pushed me so hard I gave him the side eye, but I complied with his wishes. It wasn't until the run-through of the show that I understood the process.

The show began. I was so scared. Side note: I have sung before but not on this level by myself. Terrified was not the word. *Suck it up*, I said to myself. Three of us were competing. Now let me say this: I just knew I lost. That was my thought process at the time. Performing the song, the atmosphere was just like what you see on *American Idol*. With the performance being over, I zoned out. Here I am before they announced the winner:

While waiting for the announcement of the winner, I was practicing my fake congratulations smile and clapping. Then I heard the host say, "The winner this afternoon is . . ." Then I heard, "YOLONDA!!!!!!!"

My reaction:

Since I had won, I had to do the finale show. It was one of the best shows according to the staff because all five of us could really sing, and we all sang different genres. I placed fourth, and the winner was amazing. Afterward, I took pictures with strangers and signed autographs. It was a day I will never forget. I passed out that night with a smile.

#19 Button Museum

One of my favorite pastimes is to drive. On one driving excursion, I saw a sign that said, "Button Museum." *Why would anyone have a button museum?* I mused. The tour guide started explaining the history of the museum, the founder, and the different types of buttons. She explained that there were button conferences, and the value of certain types of buttons. When I heard how much some of the buttons were worth, I wanted to search my parents' and grandparents' clothing to see if I had at least one of these buttons. One special part of the tour was toward the end. In honor of coming to the museum, you got to choose a button and glue it to their wall to commemorate your visit. Within a gigantic book, your name and the placement of your button were recorded, just in case you revisited and wanted to show off your button to your friends or family. After the tour, there was a gift shop, where I purchased a brooch made of buttons:

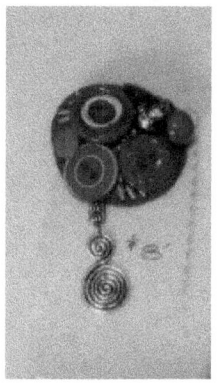

My takeaways were learning something different and discovering that people are fascinated by everything around us. If we were to open our minds, we could find a new hobby or brag about doing something so different that people will inquire about your journey.

CHAPTER 10

PERSPECTIVE

"You must be the change you want to see in the world" (Mahatma Ghandi)

What can I say? It was a fabulous journey. After my first attempt of thirty-eight things in one year, it was an emotional roller coaster. There were days I truly wanted to quit, because the pain of loss felt as big as a mountain. Days and days of wanting to quit because movement was hard. I didn't have M&M to share this journey with and get his feedback. When those great moments happened, I had a double-minded stance. Happy, because it was amazing—I never did this before. Sad, because he was the first person I wanted to call after a crazy event. Desiring to tell him how amazing it was and maybe we should try this or that. Stepping out became my new normal with different people, new friends, and often strangers to conquer my next fabulous step. More loss came in my circle, and I had to apply the same principle: "Life must go on." This statement, as I stated earlier, is easier said than done but necessary to finish the story of your life and help someone else on a similar journey. I implore you to try. Do new things. Meet different types of people. *Stretch yourself.* One may never know the amazing things you can do because you are stuck in a season. Seasons change and so will our lives. In a song I use to hate, but now embrace, "Everything Must Change," part of the lyrics states:

The young become the old,

Mysteries do unfold.

'Cause that's the way of time

Nothing and no one goes unchanged.

Winter turns to spring.

Wounded heart will heal.

Never much too soon

Everything must change

There aren't many things in life that you can be sure of..."

You may ask the question what happened after my first year of Fabulous Things. I did more wild and crazy things. Big things. Small things. I learned a lot about myself. One thing I have definitely learned about myself is that I am truly crazy. Although I was scared, I walked into it anyway, with fear at first, then confidence. Here are a few things I did after my first year:

1. Got my master's degree
2. Started a vlog/blog
3. Ziplined and rode a camel
4. Went to a talk show and was asked to be a guest (turned it down)
5. Had a belated birthday party at Medieval Times
6. Went to a Renaissance fair
7. Started singing again
8. Traveled (that's another book)

9. Started a youth group, 4YoJoy

10. Finally wrote my first book

Just to name a few. Every bold step begets another bold step. Where there some failures, absolutely, do it anyway. Do it today!!! I believe in you.

EPILOGUE

"A time to be born, and a time to die"
(Ecclesiastes 3:2)

In October and December of 2016, the most tragic things in my life happened. My father died on October 27, and five weeks later, on December 5, my baby sister unexpectantly passed away. Talk about mind-blowing, heart-wrenching, painful. Since, my experience with M&M, I understood the process of grief. It hurts . . . but my family and I are picking up the pieces of what has transpired and trudging forward into our new normal. So much has changed. We went from being a family of five. Down to four. Now to three of us, within an instant.

Right after that transpired, ironically, I did what I always wanted to do. I traveled. My family got on a plane for the first time. Our lives had been forever changed, but through God we were able to push forward. No doubt that this has been the hardest test thus far in my life, but I am living through it and not staying stuck. Is everything perfect? Absolutely not, but growth has transpired. Prayerfully, I am helping people in similar situations by living, grieving, crying, laughing, and enjoying life.

I have had so many fears of stupid things, but after the losses I have experienced, I have no reason to fear. I started my forty-fifth year with writing a book, and I will see what happens on the other side of this experience. Start your new normal by doing Fabulous Things.

BE BLESSED

JUST MISS YOLONDA

www.ingramcontent.com/pod-product-compliance
Lightning Source LLC
Chambersburg PA
CBHW052114070526
44584CB00017B/2481